More Valuable Than Gold

A collection of writings on the Miners' Strike of 1984-1985 by Striking Miners' Children

More Valuable Than Gold by Striking Miners' Children
Edited by Martin Hoyles and Susan Hemmings
Copyright rests with individual authors
Published 1985 by Martin Hoyles, 26 Oak Village, London NW5 4QN
First reprint 1985

Designed by Dianne Ceresa
Typeset by Character Typesetting Ltd, 20 Bowling Green Lane, London EC1
Printed by Blackrose Press, 30 Clerkenwell Close, London EC1 0AT

Trade distribution: Turnaround, 27 Horsell Road, London N5 1XL
and Scottish & Northern Distribution Co-operative Ltd

Price **£1.50** (postage and packing add 50p per copy)
All proceeds to **WOMEN AGAINST PIT CLOSURES**
Copies are available (by post only) from MVTG, 10 West Bank,
London N16 5DG
Cheques and postal orders payable to 'More Valuable Than Gold'

British Library Cataloguing in Publication Data
More valuable than gold
    1. English literature — 20th century
    I. Hoyles, Martin II. Hemmings, Susan
    820.8'00914   PR114B
    ISBN   0-951069-70-5

Acknowledgements

This book is largely the result of a letter written to *The Miner* in February 1985 asking for accounts of the strike from miners' children. Other contributions have come from personal contacts and particularly from Richard Burns and Norma Cohen who organised poetry workshops during the strike in Sutton-in-Ashfield and Blidworth in Notts, as part of the work of the Cambridge Miners' Support Group.

We would like to thank all those who have contributed and also those who helped collect the work, including:

Sue and Ian Bence, Aylesham, Kent
Cathrine and John Church, Bentley, S. Yorks
Martin Gostwick, editor *Scottish Miner*
Tony Green, Campsall, S. Yorks
Audrey and Matt Hall, Ashington, Northumberland
Janet Hampshire, Holmfirth, W. Yorks
Margaret Hoyles, Sheffield, S. Yorks
Deborah Knight, London
Maurice Jones, editor *The Miner*
Jeff Maddison, Doncaster, S. Yorks
Sharon Reed, Sutton-in-Ashfield, Notts
Nick Rogers, Sheffield, S. Yorks
Betty Savage, Blidworth, Notts
Doreen Selway, Abertillery, S. Wales
Brian Simons, London
Spare Rib and Local Radio Workshop
Pat Stewart, Sheffield, S. Yorks
Mary Young, Edlington, S. Yorks

Photo of Ellie Bence by Ian Steel
Illustration camerawork by Barbara Hartley
Cover drawing by Samantha Taylor, Notts

Other books on children's political concerns by the editors:
Changing Childhood ed. M. Hoyles, Writers and Readers Publishing Co-op, 1979. Collection of pieces by children and about children's political actions.

The Politics of Childhood by M. Hoyles.
Illustrated by P. Evans, Journeyman Press 1986.
Children's political struggles from a historical perspective.

Girls Are Powerful ed. S. Hemmings, Sheba 1982. Writings by girls and young women, from a feminist perspective.

True To Life ed S. Hemmings, National Association of Youth Club. Writings by girls and young women about their lives. Early 1986.

Foreword

No child from a striking miner's family could avoid being caught up in the repercussions of the past year's epic struggle. The hardship entailed by the lack of money, necessitating communal meals, the changing roles of their parents, taking part in marches, demonstrations and sometimes even picket lines, were all new experiences destined to be their vivid childhood memories in years to come. Most of all having to regard such familiar institutions as the Police, the 'telly' and even some of your neighbours and pals in an unfriendly role will be a memory difficult to completely erase. But the strike was and is about their future and it can only be a bright one if they grow up understanding the nature of working class struggle.

Betty Heathfield

Children and the miners' strike

During the 1984/5 Miners' Strike women were very involved in the campaign to stop pit closures and save the mining communities. They were active on the picket lines, organised meetings, demonstrations, national conferences, canteens, collections. They spoke at rallies all round the country. After some initial misgiving, the women's action was accepted as the backbone to the strike.

Little was said, however, about the activities of children in support of the strike. There is a general feeling that children should be shielded from the harsh realities of industrial action. They are often seen as too immature, too politically naive to know what is really going on.

It is clear from this book that this is not necessarily the case. As Cathrine Church, treasurer of Bentley Women's Action Group in Yorkshire, said, 'You will find children of all ages who actively support the strike.'

Right at the beginning of the strike there was a report on the radio that 150 Scottish pupils had walked out of school to join the miners' picket, only to be turned back by the police.

At the beginning of November 1984 some Barnsley miners came down to London to collect in Clapham. They were surprised at the generosity of Londoners and even more amazed when a group of children tipped their Guy Fawkes collection into the miners' bucket.

Miners' children invented songs such as 'We are the miners' kids' and, in good time for Xmas, 'While miners watched their pits by night'.

In September, a letter arrived from my nephew who is twelve years old and lives in Stepney:

Dear Martin

Thank you for sending me the miners' stickers. Now my school is well and truly behind the miners. But now I am short of stickers and other true blue schools have to be hit. So please can you put some more stickers in the envelope enclosed.

Yours faithfully
Oliver

In October, 80 people from Camden went to the Doncaster area to take up food, clothes and money. We met the pickets at Cortonwood and Goldthorpe and had a tremendous reception at Askern. A miner and his wife told me their thirteen-year-old daughter, Joanne, was actively supporting the strike. She later wrote me a long letter, under different headings, which is included in this book.

In Kent I met a fifteen-year-old girl called Ellie Bence. Her father is a miner at Snowdon Colliery and her mother has spent much of the strike speaking at meetings. Her grandfather was in the General Strike of 1926 and had cycled down to Kent from Scotland in 1931 to find work. Her friend Lisa, also fifteen, said she was on the picket line when both her brother and her father were arrested. They all live in the pit village of Aylesham.

Ellie had been writing poems about the strike and she told me she was going to read them out in the miners' club during a performance by the Ragged Trousered Cabaret. The cabaret commanded much attention but when Ellie got up to the mike there was complete silence. She dedicated one of the poems to her father and read it with great power and confidence:

> A job so dirty and dangerous
> Conditions worse than hell
> A stench of cold and darkness
> Is all a nose can smell
> All an ear hears is the Whistling and Banging of work
> All the men can feel is tiredness and dirt
> All the eye can see is a black and lonely cave
> Their legs and arms so heavy
> Their backs and shoulders grazed
> And when I ask my Father Why he is Striking once again
> He answers Oh So Calmly for the Unity of Men.

The final poem she sang to the tune of Amazing Grace. People stood to applaud. Her father was in tears. Ellie was overwhelmed.

> It's taken time to build our lives
> Our strong community
> But strength and love will see us through
> To keep our unity
>
> For many months we've fought like dogs
> And now the pit's a part
> Of our lives and history
> The centre of my heart
>
> As time goes on and things get hard
> I know we will pull through
> And years from now our sons will mine
> It's all the thanks to you.

Martin Hoyles

I hope as many adults as possible will buy this book for themselves (as well as for children). Don't be too ready to dismiss it as 'just' a children's book.

During the strike there was a good deal of sentimentality about children, from the left, as well as from the right and centre. This book is meant to document their own indomitable fighting spirit.

Many will say that children shouldn't be 'involved' and that if they are, they're 'indoctrinated'. Ideas about political maturity are still widely used to keep power in minority hands — we should be wary of using them towards children. It's not long since those same attitudes were used to stop women in this country 'bothering their pretty little heads' about politics.

Protecting children from life's political realities is just one way of excluding yet another group from having a say. So here they are — more valuable than gold, and twice as sparkly.

Susan Hemmings

More valuable than gold

We are the miners

We are the miners who go down the pit
With our little lamp shining and lit.
We are the miners who work all day
And we get very little pay.
We go up and down in the cage,
There are some miners very young of age.
We go home at night to our wives and families,
With the candle light burning in the corner.
Our face is black with dust
But we must, we must, we must
Go out to work for our wives and families
And keep them safe in future years to come.
Morag McGeachey, 10, Scotland

What is a miner worth?

We're fighting a losing battle
We're alone yet not afraid
We starve and we go thirsty
As a compromise is made
No one really remembers the likes of you and me
No one cares
We're the ones they do not see
Scraping for a living
Giving to the Tax Man first
Holes in our trouser pockets
But what is a Miner worth
To me he's more precious than mining
More valuable than gold
Working tiring hours
Shovelling tons of coal
So everyone please listen
It's not a lecture, just a prayer
Bosses with all their money
And us, not a penny to spare.
Ellie Bence, Kent

The pit

When will it come to an end
This strike that has starved me of the men
Who've worked my insides for ages
To earn their bread and their wages

It's dark and silent as the grave
With timbers creaking as they rot
I am now like an empty cave
Cold and wet and forgot

My roads are crumbling
My roofs fall in
Shall we ever again hear the din
Of picks and shovels working within

My belts and machines no longer humming
Only the rats and mice are running
Away from the water that's steadily
Flooding

I'm coming apart at my seams
Twists appearing in my beams
If the powers that be don't show endeavour
I'll be lost to the nation
FOREVER!

Jayne Green, 16, Yorkshire

My dad is great

My dad is great
My dad thinks of me
My dad is like a rock
He will not go back to work.

Lisa Mainwaring, 12, Nottinghamshire

Pride of a miner's daughter

To be a miner's daughter
Really makes me proud.

My dad can hold his head up high,
Not bow down to the ground.

He goes our every morning,
Picketing the pits.

My mum sometimes gets worried
In case he should get nicked.

He'd never sell his job you know,
He aims to win the fight.

He wants to work, I want to work,
We all have the right.

And one day when I'm older,
And I have got some kids,
I can look at them with pride and say,
'The Miners gave you this.'

How proud I am to have
A striking miner for a dad.

It really is much better
Than having one who is a scab!

He can always say he fought hard
To keep his job.

He didn't sell his principles
To MacGregor and his mob.

The miners are all special,
A very caring lot.

They can always say,
'We work hard for what we've got'

Donna Nicholls, 12, Yorkshire

Arthur says our mines must stay,
So listen please what he has to say.
Here is a man who understands,
If they close our pit
No more Colliery Band
Goodness knows what else will go,
The right to work, which we all know.
Of course they could all take the dole,
Never mind the fight for coal.

Could we really just sit back,
Of course we can't, our dads would be sacked.
Living thro' this long, long strike
Left us at Christmas without a bike.
It doesn't really matter tho',
Especially when the truth we know.
Rather have nothing and hold onto our pride,
You've guessed of course, we stood side by side

'OUR DAD DIDN'T SCAB'

Jennifer Scott, 11, Northumberland

Me and my dad

Me and my dad
Go in the compound
We go in very slyly
And collect bags of coal.

If the pigs see you
They will do you
They are always in blue
Ready to beat you
Between the legs.

There are four pickets at the power station
But forty-four cops
They take turns in shouting
But the cops keep on counting.

There's always one good cop
But all the others are swines
The cops come up to little ones
Ask if their daddies are on strike
And the little ones say yes
The cops turn round and say
With all their might,
'Your daddy will be in prison tonight.'
A miner's son, 14, Nottinghamshire

To be a miner

To be a miner is to stand up
Hard as iron
And don't let anything upset you
To have bone for backbone
Not jelly.
Robert Penny, 12, Nottinghamshire

I'm glad that my dad's on strike

I'm glad that my dad's on strike
Because I didn't want him crossing the picket line
I'm glad that my dad's on strike
I feel proud of him.

My dad's on strike
Because he wants to fight for our life
He's on strike
Because he's fighting for our jobs.

My mum's on strike
She's glad she's on strike
Because she goes on the picket line
Taking the pigs' numbers down
I'm glad that my mum's on strike.
Neil Gitsham, 11, Nottinghamshire

Waste a child's future

Waste a child's future
Destroy a grown man's life
Don't let him feed his children
Don't let him love his wife
A world we don't belong to
A world so cold and dark
It's a terrible, terrible place
Where the Tories have left their mark
So let's start it all from scratch
Try and live again
Forget about the Bombs
And ignore the Acid Rain
Let us go on living
Forget about the night
We'll never be defeated
The workers will unite.
Ellie Bence, Kent

England's glory

The cold, sordid morning does not deter the compassionate.
Warmth and spirit burst out like winter snowdrops.
Men of life gather by the pit gates.

Coffee fuels the live-warmth,
Fires burning second to their passion.
Cold caryatid policemen look on,
Haunted by the authority above.

Not even a King in all his splendour could equal theirs:
The miners' spirit rests within,
The power and glory of all England.

As the corrupt cage-buses sneak by
The harangue dies down.
A miner grips the cold steel fence,
Cast down in a flood of tears:
His heart frost-bitten.

But theirs is the final triumph,
They care, they are the true men of England.
And the rest of you, blinded by cliché-haunted media
Fail to see their passion.

Be like them, support them, learn from their excellence.
Look past 'uneconomic pits' and see
The miners on to victory.

Nigel Green, Yorkshire

My mum is like a butterfly

My mum is like a butterfly
My mum is like the sweetest thing on earth
My mum thinks a lot of the mineworkers.

My dad is like a sweet rose
My dad is like a rock that won't be moved
My dad is like a cupboard and the key has been thrown away.
(That means he won't go back to work, no matter how worse the matter comes and goes, the key has been thrown away so they can't move him.)

Christopher Savage, 9, Nottinghamshire

Scabs, You're daft

Scab

Scabs, you're daft, I hope you know.
Join the picket line by saying no.
You're taking the bribe of Ian MacGregor,
I thought that you would have known better.
Down the pit you drink your tea,
The problem is that you don't see.
Why do you scab?
To show off to others, that's your hobby.
Scab, you're daft, I hope you know.
Danny McNab, 10, Scotland

Backbone

A terrible thing is a scab
A scab is a terrible thing
Its backbone is made out of glass
Its brains are made out of string
It's a traitor, a coward
A thing with no conscience
It's all these things and then
The most terrible thing about scabs is
They masquerade as men.

A wonderful thing is a picket
A picket's a wonderful thing
His back is strong and proud
He uses his brain to think
He is brave, he's courageous
He looks to the future
He's all these things and plus
The most wonderful thing about pickets is
That they belong to us.
Jane Petney, 14, Nottinghamshire

Life in Blidworth

Life in Blidworth is very dull
There are scabs lurking in the dark alleys
Ashamed of their attitudes

They should all come out
And join the strike
And then it will end very soon

All the families are depressed
And so are the children
Some children enjoy more than others (scabs)

The strike centre is a pleasant place
Where people join to play
And fathers play cards
And have a happy time

And the wives cook the meals
For the children and the men.
Christopher Savage, 9, Nottinghamshire

Steven Dorsey, 9, Nottinghamshire

Scabs

My father's a man who works very hard
He's proud of his job and his Union Card
But Scabs bring disgust, disgust and shame
On the working class
And the Mining Game
So come on you Scabs
Come and join us
Let's earn a living
In a future to trust
Let's show the people
The Miners are best
We want a future
We want nothing less
Let us Unite, We can survive
Let's show them we are Alive
A future to live in
A future to keep
A job to go to
To make ends meet
A future that's ours
Forever and more
A future that's there
Something to live for
So come on you Scabs
Come and join us
For a job in the future
A job we can trust.
Ellie Bence, Kent

Here lies

Here lies the body of Billy Dab
Pity is he was a scab
The pickets stood and called his name
And finally he died . . . of shame.
Jayne Petney, 14, Nottinghamshire

A picket

A picket is like a man with no money
Some days he is very funny.

A wife of a picket is very hard working
They are searching and searching for food to eat.

A child of a picket is very good
You get parties and things and all things good.
Kerri Starr, 8, Nottinghamshire

My dad is good, my dad is bad

My dad is good, my dad is bad
But I can tell you one thing
My dad is not a scab.

My mum is good
But sometimes she can get very mad
But there is one thing
She will not led dad be a scab.
Brendan Reed, 9, Nottinghamshire

It's not easy being a scab

It's not easy being a scab
Or a blackleg, so it's called
I'd rather be a picket
Or something of that sort
I'd like to be with all my mates
On the picket line
But my wife threatened to leave me
If I did not toe the line
So now I've had to change my mind
A scab I shall remain
Each morning I go into work
I hang my head in shame.

Jane Cassattarie, 13, Nottinghamshire

Jingle bells

Jingle bells

Jingle bells, jingle bells
Jingle all the way
I would rather be a picket
Than a scab on Christmas Day.

My dad was on strike for one year
And it was very hard for us down here
We have many scabs and Tories too
Who did not want us to see it through
But we, the kids, we showed them all
We supported our dads and stood six foot tall
We went on rallies and marches too
We told the world, 'Scargill, we support you.'

There were times when it was hard at school. They made fun of me and said I would not get much for Christmas. But I would go through it all again.
Jason Cheetham, 11, Wales

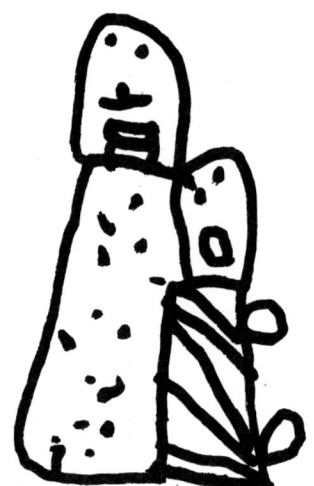

Winter

Winter is the king
Of showmen
Turning snowflakes
Into snowmen
Turning houses
Into birthday cakes.
Danny Jones, 8, Nottinghamshire

Christmas at the Strike Centre

On Christmas morning we woke up and went downstairs and opened the living-room door. We went through and saw a lot of presents in wrapping paper. We went and sat on the carpet and took a present each and we opened them if they had our names on. After we had opened them we threw the wrapping paper away. After we had opened them we played with them. At about 9.30 my mum came up the strike centre and helped the other women cook the dinner and lay the tables. We played at home until 12.30 and then we came up and found a seat for our dinner. There was wine and cigarettes for the grown-ups and orange for the children. At 3 o'clock Father Christmas came and gave all the children a sack full of toys and we all had a game or something from France. I got a modelling set of cowboys and indians. All the men got a present too — they got two pairs of socks. The ladies got a present too — it was a box of chocolates and a bottle of perfume. When Santa had given out all the presents we all had a party and a fancy dress. I dressed up as a punk, so did Karen. After we had had our party we went home and watched TV.
On Boxing Day we came up the centre and had a big dinner again.
Helen Taylor, 10, Nottinghamshire
P.S. We enjoyed it.

Christmas

When I got up I had lots of presents. My mum said do you like your toy. I said yes thank you. We came up to the strike centre and had our dinner and we had a sack full of toys and we had the best time ever. We played and played and then we went home and we played upstairs and had a bath and we played till 8 o'clock. We were very happy and then we watched some TV and went to bed. My mum came upstairs with us and gave us a kiss and we went to sleep. Boxing Day was good too. We were playing with our toys. We were very happy. We went up the strike centre. I love it at Christmas. It was very good. It was lovely. I was happy all Christmas. It was very nice.
Samantha Taylor, 8, Nottinghamshire

Heart they have not

Mr MacGregor can't you see
That we're not so greedy
All we want is to save our pit
But you won't give in just one little bit
You take our food you take our money
While you sit at No 10 drinking champagne and eating honey.

Christmas is near but we've no fear
We'll last out the good new year
Maggie sends out her boys in blue
While our pickets stand steady and true
The blue stormtroopers carry on
We'll fight and clash and stand to the last
Until the pickets are stopped being harassed.

Jason Stewart, 7, Yorkshire

Old MacGregor had a plan

Old MacGregor

Old MacGregor had a plan
Hee I, hee I, ho.
Under this plan pits would go
Hee I, hee I, ho.
With a boo, boo here
And a boo, boo there
Here boo, there boo, everywhere a boo, boo.

Old MacGregor has no mind
Hee I, hee I, ho.
Maggie pulls his strings
Hee I, hee I, ho.
With a pull, pull here
And a pull, pull there
Here pull, there pull, everywhere a pull, pull.

Old MacGregor had a shock
Hee I, hee I, ho.
The miners stood up and fought back
Hee I, hee I, ho.
With a roar, roar here
And roar, roar there
Here roar, there roar, everywhere a roar, roar.

The Police also had a scheme
Hee I, hee I, ho.
To stop the strikers was their theme
Hee I, hee I, ho.
With a chase, chase here
And a chase, chase there
Here chase, there chase, everywhere a chase, chase.

Old MacGregor went into hibernation
Hee I, hee I, ho.
His disappearance did not kid the nation
Hee I, hee I, ho.
With a laugh, laugh here
And a laugh, laugh there
Here laugh, there laugh, everywhere a laugh, laugh.

Old MacGregor will soon get the sack
Hee I, hee I, ho.
Maggie will also go, this is a fact
Hee I, hee I, ho.
With a cheer, cheer here
And a cheer, cheer there
Here cheer, there cheer, everywhere a cheer, cheer.
Dean Selway, 11, Wales

Scargill Poems
1
Scargill is like a god that walks on water
Scargill is the god of the pickets
He supports us well as we support him
He's like an emperor of the pickets
Scargill lives on
When Scargill dies, he will live on
Through the National Union of Mineworkers.
Neil Gitsham, 11, Nottinghamshire

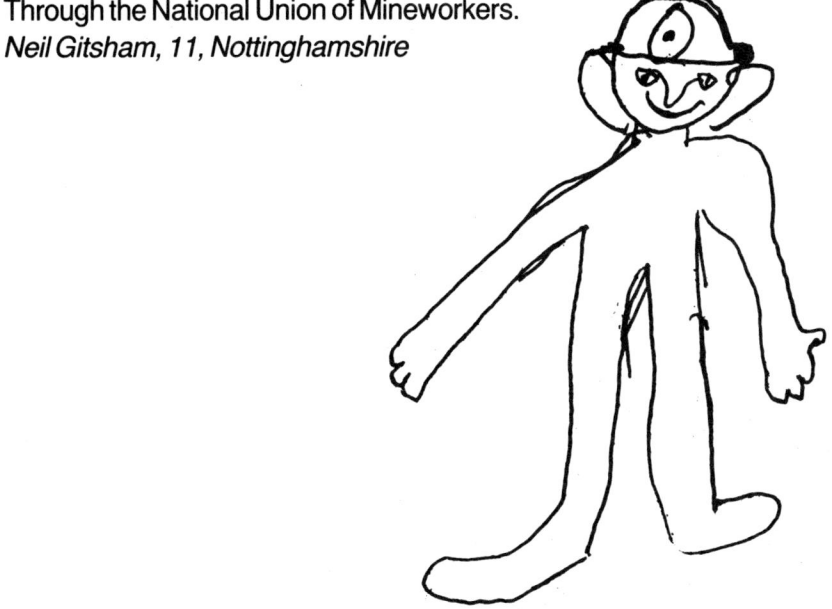

2

Scargill is like a king to us
He's the King of Pickets
He supports us and helps us to win
Scargill is a magic man
He never gets battered or beat
We all support the mighty Scargill
He's the bestest man.
Lee Mainwaring, 10, Nottinghamshire

3

Scargill is like a Pro man
Scargill is like the best
Scargill is like the King of the Universe
Without Scargill we wouldn't be able to manage
Without Scargill we wouldn't be able to win
Scargill is a Peace man.
Christopher Savage, 9, Nottinghamshire

4

Scargill is like a coal king
Scargill is like a supporter
We and Scargill get on well together
Scargill does not get on with scabs
Scargill will win the dispute.
Phillip Robottom, 10, Nottinghamshire

5

Scargill is like a God of the Heavens
Caring for pickets, families, future and mankind
He is a leader and must not be forgotten
He is the saviour for all our pits
Scargill is like a lion, so brave
Seeing the future, who Thatcher delays
He is a man hopeful of winning
The emerald of pickets, the treasure of the future
With Scargill guiding, WE MUST WIN
Scargill lives on.
Paul Dove, 13, Nottinghamshire

The letter

I've written a letter to Maggie
Her address is 10 Downing Street
I've written a letter to tell her
That the miners will never be beat.

So get off your backside dear Maggie
Can't you see we're winning the FIGHT
Because all the unions are with us
To stand for the just and the right.

You've tried to starve us dear Maggie
How cruel can anyone be
But you'll never succeed dear Maggie
For united we have the key.

To stand and confront you dear Maggie
As we know when this day is through
We'll win the right to work
And that will be goodbye to you!
Kerry Adele Evans, 12, Wales

Knowing what we're talking about

The strike

This strike means a lot to me and my dad because he and all other men who are on strike are fighting against job losses and for their children's future. Although I am eleven I understand most of the strike. I like going on the picket line with my mum and dad and friends, and the boys in blue watching us. Also going on marches holding placards with COAL NOT DOLE and SAVE JOBS. Some of my mates' dads are on strike and we get along well. I've made new friends while the strike's been going on. I think we all have a chance of winning. I hope you will give us all the support you can, for we want to show Maggie up. She can't always win.
Leanne Platek, 11, Staffordshire

We want a future

I just see myself as a miner's daughter. That's political enough for me. It's been terrible at school because most of the teachers — I'd say 80% — are conservative. There's only a few that understand what's going on, politically and everything. Then there's been quite a few teachers belittling miners' children in front of the class. Recently there was a third year girl who had a 'Kent women against pit closures' tee-shirt on and this very conservative teacher made her take it off. Then he got her up in front of the class and he said, 'How much is your father getting? What do you think about the strike?' And for a thirteen-year-old girl it's ever such a frightening experience, especially coming from someone so much older than you. But they don't ask me or my friends 'cos we're a lot older and we really understand and we know how to answer. They make us take our badges off. I understand that, when they're on your school uniform, but when they're on your bags or your coat I don't really think they've got the right. But no one asks me to take my badges off, because I've got a bigger mouth than everyone else and I tell them where to get off! The teachers really get at the younger children though, more than the older ones, really picking on them all the time. Now they're on about the uniform, saying you're not allowed to wear tee-shirts any more, you've got to wear shirts, which is really stupid cos they know you can't afford to go out and buy a shirt for seven pounds whereas you can get a tee-shirt for two pounds.

I remember when I was younger, six or seven, I always wanted to go down the pit, cos my grand-dad used to talk about it, and it used to fascinate me. Every year the school used to take the boys down on a trip. Next term I'm going to fight to let the girls go down. I know it'd be hard work, but six months ago there was a programme about American women working down the mines. I thought if they can do it over there, I reckon I can do it. I've always had admiration for miners, the men in my family's always worked down the mines, and I've great respect for them. This will be the strike that no one will ever forget. The '72 strike was important, but this, the future depends on it. I think it's

Ellie Bence reading her work

brought us closer together, there's been less arguments between the whole family and everyone's really trying to help. We all understand the difficulties with money. We've cut back a bit on food and everything. But we're getting by. In the village, everyone's gotten so much closer now. It's nice, like no one argues with their mum and dad any more. And we've stopped asking for pocket money. My friend said, 'Well, I can't go down the youth club cos it's not right asking me mum for money when she hasn't got it.' There's less money going around for children and so we go to less places, but we're always together now. Just walking around the street, laughing and joking really. But when you do start talking, the main topic of conversation is the strike. You'll always get a few children, maybe from out of the village who don't really know what you're talking about and they try to be clever. And then you've got maybe twenty children who know what they're talking about against two children that don't. And they chat to them for about ten minutes and they see the light. They finally understand.

Aylesham sticks out terribly in Kent because we're like a big red dot in the middle of a big blue sheet. People just can't understand and accept that we in Aylesham think differently to them. It's terrible really, you'd be talking to someone and they'd say, 'Where do you come from?' And you'd say 'Aylesham.' Their response is, 'Ah well, I've got to go now.' It's like that all the time.

33

It's the way of the village, it's just accepted that the lads go down the pits and women work at the factories. It's always been that way. We're fighting so that we'll still have the choice whether to go down the pit or not. That's about the only thing that is available, cos a few factories have closed down at the industrial estate. If the pits did close, I think that'd be the end of the village really. People say why don't you move away and that, but there's nowhere to move to, everyone's got their own problems. You always get a few bad apples in the barrel, but the people outside the village seem to think we're all bad, that there's nothing good. It's a shame, cos I can't see anything bad about us, so I'd never move away from Aylesham. There's never been really a sort of warm feeling between the people of the village and police before, but now it's just hatred. Whenever you see a police car or a policeman you just swear under your breath. They've always been out to get us. Just before the strike it started to get a little better, but now it's worse. It's not the person we dislike, it's because the person is a police officer. It's a shame really, cos there is one policeman in the village and he really tries to get in with the kids and everything. And he's not known as PC whatever, he's known as Andy the copper. But we'll never forgive the police for what they've been doing. The way they've brought our fathers down. Out of everyone in the village I can only think of two that have become policemen.

There's been a few television programmes about the village and what makes me sick is that they always take the shots in the pub or where women are playing bingo. They never take a camera to the playgroup or to the school at breakfast. I remember the first miner that was killed on the picket line was only briefly mentioned on the news once. Then a few weeks later, when Yvonne Fletcher was killed, they had her parents and colleagues talking on the television about what a saintly figure she was. And she might have been, for all I know, but they only said there was a picket killed today and made it sound as if he was crushed by the crowd. That's why I'm angry with the media. With the Nottinghamshire miners as well, they say so many are going to work. They never say how many are on strike, or they say the pit's working, or partially working, but they don't say that loads aren't working.

I can't bring myself to watch the television now, or read the papers. It's really maddening to just have to sit there and listen to a pack of lies. The support the miners are getting really cheers me up. You go out of the village and you see posters saying 'Victory to the Miners'. You feel like saying 'Look at that poster over there!' even if you're not with anybody. It's funny, before the strike, you'd just think that's a nice badge, but now you spot one miles away, 'Oh, they've got a sticker on, great!'
Ellie Bence, Kent

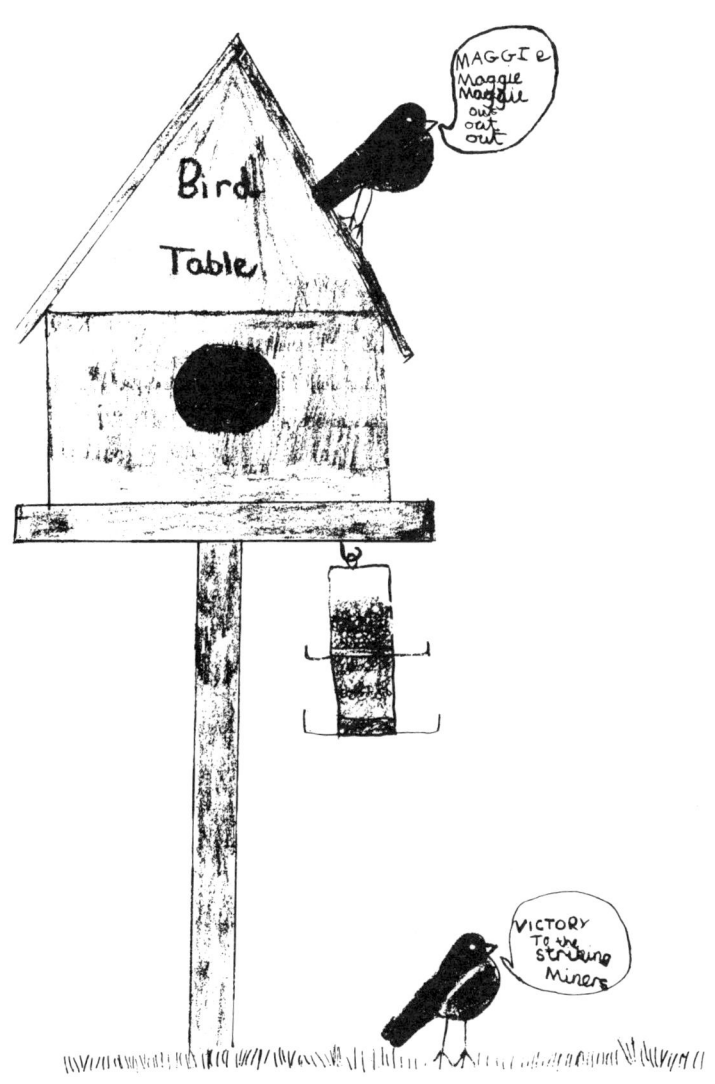

Susan Sandhu, 8, Nottinghamshire

Monday 25 February 1985

Yesterday I went on a march to London and it took four hours to get there and when we got there I got off the bus. We went in the park with our banner. There was lots and lots of people there and they all had banners. The banners had lanes. We was lane four. Then we had to listen to some people talking on a lorry and then we started to march. We had a bucket and we was marching round the streets asking for money, but then one of the policemen said it's against the law for people under eighteen to be collecting money. Arthur Scargill was in the march. We went past Mrs Thatcher's house and we all booed. When we got to the square we put the banner down and we listened to Arthur. Then we went back and there was police blocking the road and we had to go round them. We got lost on the way so we had to go and ask the cops. We went past Buckingham Palace and then when we got to the bus it was not there so we had to wait. Then it came and we was singing songs all the way home.

Kirsty Rankin, 7, Yorkshire

Saturday's march and rally

Saturday morning up early today,
    Cos we've got to travel quite a way,
Meet the coach at half past seven,
    Arriving in London way after eleven.
The march started near the Thames waters,
    The London streets were lined with all our supporters.
We handed in a petition from 3,000 plus,
    For all the money the government owe us.
Round the corner and on for three and a half miles,
    All the people marching wear brave smiles.
After a couple of hours we reach the end of the walk,
    Where some union leaders give a solidarity talk.
We return from the march to Camden Town Hall,
    Where a hot meal is waiting free for all.
So if it wasn't for Camden, the Labour Party too,
    Bentley simply don't know what they'd do.

Mark Potts, 13, Yorkshire

The strike

While my dad picketed to stop them closing the pits, I helped my mam at our jumble sales to raise money. We had nice times on our trips with the union to the beach and parks, and we made lots of new friends. Uncle Derek used to make us laugh and sing songs. I missed our colour television. We had to watch a black and white set. At Christmas we had a smashing party and we got lovely toys sent from France. I wrote a letter thanking the people who sent us the presents. I am pleased my dad is now back at work after twelve months on strike.

Nicola Cowan, 8, Northumberland

> Ollerton Miners Welfare ON One Sunday in 1984
>
> ICE CREAM VAN
>
> LOLLY POP
>
> My Grandpa and Daddy and their friends collect money for Striking miners children to have free ice-cream.

Susan Sandhu, 8, Nottinghamshire

37

Me and my thoughts of the miners' strike

It was half way through the strike when things started to get worse in Edlington (Doncaster). I couldn't believe how police treated striking miners. When my dad used to go picketing every day at Nottingham and places all over England, he used to tell my mam how police treated them, especially when my dad spent a week in Blidworth (Nottingham), and how you couldn't move about without police following them. But when they came to my village it made me realize what these striking miners had been through. It makes me very proud of these striking miners.

Two months before the strike ended, that's when the trouble at Edlington Comprehensive School started. It was a Monday afternoon and a load of school kids were standing at the gates singing and shouting for people to come out on strike, so I decided to join them. After the second day on strike it ended out to be that six were excluded, then two were let back in. After a meeting of the Governors three were expelled and I was the only one let back in.

I feel very proud of the striking miners who stuck the strike out and I wish they could have stayed out till they had won. I feel very sorry for the families of the striking miners who got killed through the strike.

Pam McCann, 15, Yorkshire

> **Pit village schoolgirls suspended**
>
> FOUR pit village schoolgirls have been suspended after picketing their comprehensive in South Yorkshire.

I am a miner's son

I am a miner's son
That means I have to come to the strike centre for my dinner
That means my dad helps other people
That means my mum does all the shopping
That means my sister cries all the time
And our family get on well, good all together.

Danny Jones, 8, Nottinghamshire

'Media' — true or false?

As I come from a miner's family, my views on the miners' strike will favour the *striking* miners. When the miners' strike first started was back in October 1983. Four pits from this area started an overtime ban. The four pits were Manvers Colliery, Kilnhurst Colliery, Wath Colliery and Cadeby Colliery. A full national strike happened on February 20th 1984. Most areas went on strike immediately, apart from the Nottingham area. Slowly Nottingham workers came out on strike, but the rest stood firm. Heavy picketing began. Violence started and so heavy policing began. Soon violence got even worse. This is when the press and television reports started telling the public of the violence that occurs on most pickets. Immediately the pickets get the blame. Some newspapers (Tory) totally back Mr MacGregor, some newspapers back the miners' strike. I think the TV reports are sometimes fair, but the newspapers are not. Independent newspapers are formed such as 'The Miner Special Issue'. This newspaper brings stunning articles on violence on picketing and also some stunning photos. This newspaper is biased towards the miners. I read one article that the Government was using soldiers on the picketing, but the Government denied this. Here are two photographs from 'The Miner':

John Harris (IFL)

Is this behaviour really necessary? Luckily this woman was missed by the charging policeman. This picture was not shown in any public newspaper or on any TV programme or news. Can you see how the woman would nearly have been struck on the back? Probably this woman would have been warned of the galloping horse and rider.

39

My dad and his friend have never seen anybody being struck on the front of the body, but all the truncheon marks are on the back of the body. This proves when somebody is struck they are going to be struck on the back. They would not have seen the oncoming blow.

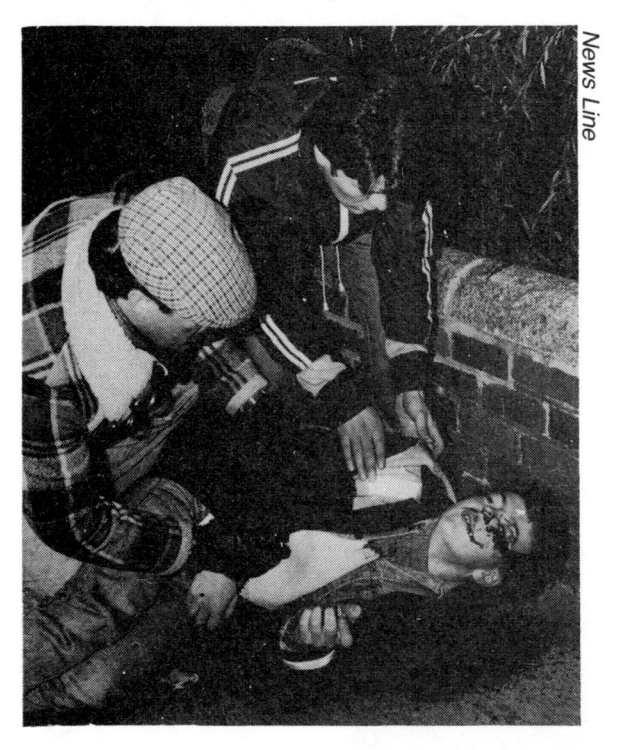

News Line

This picture shows the bias against the pickets. 'Frickley Colliery's Darren Price — knocked down by a police horse box as it deliberately mounted the pavement, and then run over by a police Transit van. In hospital it was discovered that his jaw had been broken. *Again, such pictures were carefully censored out of the national media.'*

The reason why pictures like these are not shown on the public screen or in national newspapers is because the government doesn't want the public to see disturbing scenes that are caused by police and pickets, because the government controls most television programmes.

If scenes like this were shown on television the public would soon change their views on the terrible dispute. And the government says they 'don't involve themselves in the dispute'! Some miners think that the dispute will end this coming winter with more miners returning to work, but this seems unlikely. This dispute has taught us a great deal.

Wayne Oldfield, 16, Yorkshire

The strike

My father, Henry Daley, works at Nostell Colliery (North Yorkshire) and is chairman of the North Yorkshire Area NUM. He has been on strike for eleven and a half months, since 12 March 1984. I am 15 years old and these are my views at the time of writing, 18 February 1985.

From the very start I have supported *all* striking miners. I still do. I do not, and cannot, support the fighting which is not only on picket lines. I do not know anyone who does. Why, therefore, have there been horrible, un-needed and unjust scenes of violence on and off the picket lines. All this does is make the NUM lose public support — this support is what they desperately need. Attacks on working miners should never take place. The ordinary miner never got balloted. They have a right to speak up, and it is easily understood why men are returning to work.

In my view the strike has been lost by the NUM. Even the NCB has lost too much to claim victory. The NUM has lost against an ever-increasing right-wing capitalist government.

The NUM now have to conduct their affairs in such a manner as to avoid panic, division and weakness in the face of the coal board. They would do this best by staying together and staying united in the defence of the union. Every time someone returns to work this undermines the union and strengthens the coal board.

I believe this strike is now nearing its end. If this is so the NUM need to press for speedy negotiations to bring about an organised return to work so that the miners can take advantage of tax-free wages and holiday pay to be had before 5 April.

The National Executive Committee of the NUM should NOW get an organised settlement enabling all the members to go back to work TOGETHER. The NUM members must not crawl back to work. They must return as they left: TOGETHER. The men have pits to run when they are back at work. The pits belong to the miners. If they fragment themselves in the return they perpetuate that fragmentation in their production capacities. If the NUM are to attract capital development, as they want, then they must show team-work and unity. This cannot be done when men desert the union and ally themselves with the coal board. That is something that ought to be considered by men returning to work. Without team-work there will be no investment.

The NUM are facing a no-win situation. That is quite obvious. That is why the NEC should make sure negotiations continue and obtain terms rather than be defeated and have terms imposed on them.

The miners may be DOWN but they are not OUT. Very few pits in the Yorkshire area are producing coal. While the NUM have the support of NACODS they have a strong card. It hurts the board that they cannot use those at work on underground activities. Why, then, should an NUM member cross a picket line when deputies are turning back home?

Finally — the best means to achieve something positive is by standing together. The best means to protect themselves in the event of a defeat is also by standing together. There is no other way. This dispute has been the hardest dispute ever seen. The NUM members should come out of this with dignity, not shame. They should come out of this as men, not as coal board lackeys. Everyone, except the government it seems, wants this strike ending.

We all understand why men are returning to work. The members of the NUM should now stand together and press the NEC for a settlement which takes the NUM back together. This will leave the striking miners with a union to go to.

The NUM should make sure that the end of this strike is one that in 20 years time people like my father can say: WE DID IT RIGHT rather than one they are ashamed to talk about.

The only success for the NUM is now for men to STAND TOGETHER in defence of our great union and the trade union movment. They should stay out on strike and be proud for what they have done. The NUM needs striking miners.

Whatever people say or do to me about my father and his striking colleagues there is one thing they cannot take away — the pride I have for my father. I am still supporting the strike after nearly one year. I wish I could say the same for some members of the NUM who are working.

Andrew Daley, 15, Yorkshire

The miners' strike

It started in February '84
And ended in March '85
And the twelve months that were between them
Was one of the worst years of my life.

Miner turned against miner
And families were split in two
The anger and bitterness upset me
But there was nothing I could do.

The policemen were pigs I started to think
I'd never hated them so
When they took their truncheons and started to charge
I just wanted them to go.

When dad went on the picket line
Each and every day
I couldn't wait till he got home
I wanted him to stay.

I didn't want him going out
In case he might get hurt

I was worried about the violence
The police treated them like dirt.

I hoped he wouldn't be arrested
I don't know what I'd have done
But he didn't and luckily he didn't get hurt a lot
He's one in a million.

The scabs I wished I could kill them
And I wished Maggie Thatcher dead
I've never wished that on anyone
So I wished it on the scabs instead.

All the policemen started to move
From their homes to a new estate
I'm glad they all moved cos I hated them
Anyway most of them couldn't wait.

We found out two scabs lived down the avenue
I wanted to prove their decision was wrong
But someone told me not to worry:
'They'll not have their windows for long.'

My aunt and uncle were helpful
They gave us money and chocs
I was grateful to them
I soon filled my money box.

I was able to buy some new clothes
I felt sorry for those who couldn't
They had to get clothes from jumble sales
And social security, I wouldn't.

I was relieved when the strike was ended
But when they marched back I was sad
Dad and the miners were full up with tears
The strike had been only one thing, bad.

Jill Gaskell, 14, Yorkshire

Nicky Platek, 9, Staffordshire

Why did we fall apart and how did we come back together?

It all started about a year ago. The atmosphere in the house was cheerful and happy as usual. As March 1984 approached, my dad began to bring up his occupation in most conversations. Often while I was reading in bed at night I would hear the more private conversation between my mum and dad. They never did mention much to me about it, but as the time drew a lot nearer I was soon to be in for a mighty shock. Truthfully it was more like a blow to the head. Yes of course I'm talking about the strike. The Miners' Strike of 84/85.

The first few months were all right. Well, with the exception of margarine instead of butter (one thing I noticed straight away) things all seemed to be running smoothly. My dad had just got his allotment and was planting vegetables. These vegetables on a small plot of land became the essential protein in our diets for the next twelve months. The year my dad was striking seemed a never-ending nightmare. About the first two months I didn't really think about it in any other way, only that I was proud that my dad and all the other miners would make sacrifices to save pits and thousands of jobs. What followed changed my opinion. Hundreds of news reports, interviews with a man named Arthur Scargill. A year or so ago anyone who said to me, 'Do you know Arthur Scargill did so and so the other day?' I would probably have said, 'Arthur what? Who's he?' But this has made me realise Arthur Scargill, although he failed this time, is a man of bloody steel. It's made me more aware of politics. A while ago I would have rather turned to a Beano or watch Playschool than sit and listen to 'her': 'her' being Mrs T, Mrs Thatcher the so-called 'Iron Lady'. While the situation with the strike was on, I was glued to the little square box. Even if I was to jeer and contradict I'd listen with interest.

The most distressing parts in our family were the pain, the arguments and my selfish guilt. I got my so-called nickname 'Dawn the wanter' ages ago. It was because nearly every day I'd say to mum, dad or anyone in earshot, 'I want this', 'I want that'. My dad replied many times with, 'You'll get some of this if you don't shut up'. I retreated nervously as he had up his fist. Before the strike our family got on okay, but 'okay' is only the word to describe it. I mean I couldn't say we all got on fantastically as I'd be a born liar, what with my brothers, one of who is twenty-seven, unemployed for five years, and the other is thirty, working and getting along fine. They didn't speak to each other for five years after a personal argument leading to a vicious fight. I call myself selfish because I never took no notice of the fact that my brother was getting more depressed each day. After about seven months of the strike I did, as we all did, get concerned, for my brother turned to alcohol to solve his problems. This was then followed by continuous drinking and by a nervous breakdown and a hospital bed in a ward for alcoholics. Several visits were made by a psychiatrist as no way would he go to that hospital, he refused to go. Partly I don't blame him. He's so full of knowledge and is very intelligent. He usually now reads and passes time in the library. Fortunately now after sleeping tablets and valium have been fed into his system he's calmed down and off the tablets and almost certainly recovering. He gets depressed, but in moderation as each and every one of us do.

Mum, she's great, a cheerful person with so much patience. I take after her for that. She's cooked up some gorgeous meals and almost led us to believe we were eating caviare and then steak. Underneath her happy smile there's a woman who's suffering badly, in pain constantly. For my mum has bad arthritis to the spine. She must wear a surgical corset. So I've been helping as much as I can, cooking, cleaning, joking. When mum and me go shopping I see her face frown, the tired eyes dreaming, as at the checkout she sees the woman in front spending fifty or sixty pounds on shopping. I could cry as she looks at the half empty trolley and the ten pound note in her hand. I'd love her to be happy. Luckily my boyfriend cheers my mum up so much. He is only on a YTS and earning fifty pounds a fortnight. Automatically twenty-five pounds goes to his mother, ten in a deposit account, five for club money and five to his dad which is money he has to borrow. What a life, but still he practically bought me my fifth year uniform. He's a brilliant person and he is very special, not just to me, to us all.

Dad did go out a lot before the strike. He often went for a drink but after the strike he had to settle for homebrew kits. These died down and he eventually had to do with nothing. This made him moody, stroppy and, as the money ran out, very irritable. My other brother works at Danish Bacon. He's bought mum lovely things. Not clothes or a bottle of wine nor cigarettes — my mum doesn't drink, smoke or dress up and she rarely goes out anywhere. But he brings her whopping cuts of meat — beef, pork and lamb, chickens and such. I never ask. I never ask for anything now. My sisters are great too. All three are happily married with children, one blessing at least. They bring us lovely food too, chocolate chip cookies, a change from boring plain ones. My favourite too — wholemeal bread. I hate white packaged bread, why it tastes more like putty.

Me, I've changed. I've realised money isn't everything in this world. Okay it's quite something to be rich and never short, but when you do go short you'll know happiness and love can never be bought.

The worst thing was school. I had to go on listening to stupid girls saying, 'The strike's pathetic', 'I don't know what they're striking for' and, 'I'm sick of hearing about it.' If only they knew the atmosphere in my house, it was so icy you could cut it with a knife. Also when they talk about the lovely clothes, computers, bikes and money they got from their parents for Christmas, I could have cried. More than likely I was crying inside, crying because for Christmas there were not lovely clothes, leather coats and no this and that for me. I could have ripped their eyes out with jealousy. But I had a better present than them all. I had love and comfort from my boyfriend and my family. The little I got from relatives was far better than any clothes and computers. I got a feeling I was needed and my help was appreciated. I can understand any mining family and I know now what it must be like for any one-parent family. The fear and the pride being torn from you like when you have to enter the education welfare office for a coat. I felt like a scrounger and after I came out of the office I cried, I cried violently. My mum too was upset to see my unhappiness, my torturous torment, her upset thinking somehow my career would be ruined. No, not me I'm afraid, I've got determination, I've got the push to do and be what I want. I will get somewhere, I know, even if I have to start at the bottom. Some day I'll repay my parents the kindness I owe them. I'll return something to my boyfriend to whom I owe so much for keeping me going, keeping me fighting.

Now the strike's over there's no time for rejoicing, just the bills, the rent, the hundreds of pounds we owe, almost reaching four figures. My teenage years won't be fancy-free, but all down to the true grit, hard graft. But believe me I'm not the sort of person to give in and I swear to god I won't.

Dawn Newton, 15, Yorkshire

The struggle for survival

The struggle for survival
It all started off in '83
When the Tories proclaimed their final decree.

Ten months have past,
Not a single word,
No sign of a settlement,
Nothing is heard.

Nights draw on, day by day,
Their poor little faces filled with dismay,
Their innocent minds, their hearts, their fate,
Not aware that the Tories are digging their grave.

So stand up and fight,
Play it all fair,
Help the young ones,
Show that you care.

Where has all the feeling gone
That once was strong,
Lost in hatred — one by one.

So let's all pull together,
Let's rid of the Tory,
Fight and win —
And then claim the glory.

Here in Yorkshire, and everywhere else for that matter, the strike is over, but the dispute isn't. The Coal Board and Government haven't won by a long chalk! The miners are still fighting, in South Yorkshire everyone is pulling together and are solid and united. I have always said since the beginning of the dispute that the miners will win a victory and fight for the right to work. Even if there is ever a major revolutionary reaction, where everyone comes out on strike, such as miners, steelworkers, railway men, seamen, nurses, university students, teachers etc. I think this country needs a revolution, if only to prove that Maggie Thatcher will *not* take away our freedom and we all stand up and fight for what is rightfully ours, a major revolution is what this country needs to get Britain back on its feet.

Lesley Kirkwood, 15, Yorkshire

They've sacked my dad
They've sacked my dad you know
Though he'd done nothing wrong
They've sacked him cos he was on strike
On strike for far too long
They found him innocent you know
The judge was rather cross:
'This man should not have got the sack.'
So my dad went and told his boss.
'I'm innocent,' my father said,
'It's proved I did no wrong.'
But yes he had, he'd been on strike
On strike for far too long
They've sacked my dad you know
But I am proud of him.
Jayne Petney, 14, Nottinghamshire

Proud to take part
Recently my father had his last panel meeting as chairman of the North Yorkshire Area NUM, before his retirement. He was presented with a gold watch and hammer and gavel, with a fifty pence indented in the case. This is what he used to keep order during the strike. During the presentation he made a speech thanking his colleagues and mentioning the strike. He said, and I quote: 'If I had been offered £20,000 — instead of the £4,000 I'm being offered now as redundancy payment — during the strike I would not have accepted it. I would have given anything to say I was part of the historic struggle, even though I knew we would lose, and I am proud, along with my good friends and colleagues at the North Yorkshire panel, to be able to say I took part in the strike of 1984/85 and I DID IT RIGHT by NOT returning to work.'

I, like him, would have given anything to take part in the strike, and I did, getting food parcels ready for Crofton miners and going on rallies. I supported the miners who stayed out to the end and were brought closer together. We had a party at Christmas-time, and I did not for one moment feel sorry for myself because I would not get any presents. I never went without though.

I had great friendship, and support for what I did. At Christmas the strike brought certain members of our community closer together than they had ever been before — all because they believed in what they were doing, because it was right — fighting for a job, not just for themselves, but also for the future. I have not supported our leadership totally throughout the strike, only the NUM, but I have never looked back and regretted, nor will I ever, the fact that I played a part in the greatest strike of all time — the NUM strike of 1984/85.
Andrew Daley, 16, Yorkshire

Bentley, The strike of '84

Miners on the picket lines,
   Deserted now, once working mines.
MacGregor and Scargill fight it out,
   The coppers don't half pack a clout.
Free dinners in the pavilion hall,
   At the weekend we play cricket and football.
They talk for hours on end,
   But not a thing do they mend.
Camden give support which we so badly need,
   They help Bentley miners of every colour, kin or creed.
Flying pickets from the Yorkshire Coalfield,
   Truncheons are what coppers wield.
Scabs keep working, protected by the fuzz,
   Prolonging the dispute is all this does.
The Strikers struggle through the pit war,
   Never to forget the strike of '84.

Bentley, The strike of 84-85

Picketing the pit twice a day,
   For the miners on strike there is no pay.
Send the Yankee back to where he belongs,
   Because the strike is all he prolongs.
Families struggle to keep their heads above water,
   It's MacGregor we should slaughter.
Camden visit us once in a while,
   They send us money by the pile.
When you feel moody and have got the colour blue,
   The Action Group come and pull you right through.
No money do the families have to spend,
   We all wonder when the strike will end.
The women serve dinners in array,
   They feed so many in a day.
The strikers struggle to survive,
   They won't forget 1984-85.

Mark Potts, 13, Yorkshire

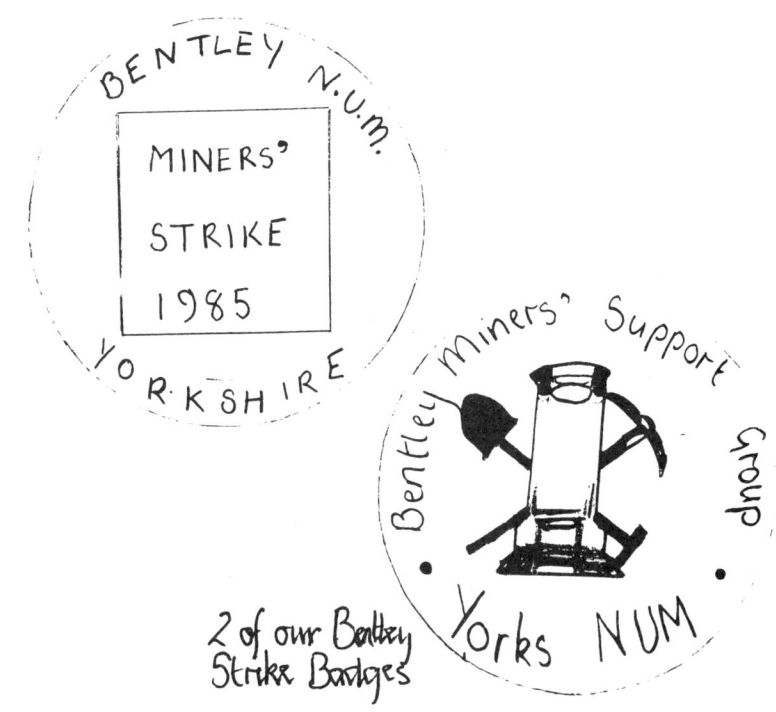

2 of our Bentley Strike Badges

Mark Potts, 13, Yorkshire

How the miners strike has affected me

The miners' strike has affected me in many ways because my dad is a miner and since the strike has been on, I have not been able to go out as much because I have not had enough money and I have not been able to buy any new clothes or any new records. I have had to save up all my money that other relatives have given me so that I can go swimming and go out a few times. This year none of our family has been on holiday because we have not had enough money and I have really missed a holiday.

When I am in the house sometimes I have arguments with my dad because I can't go out and then I always blame him for not being at work and me not being able to go out because I never have any money. Then my mum will sometimes get involved and my mum and dad witll start arguing. My mum will say that she has to go out and earn all the money for us to make a living and tells my dad that he should get back to work, but really she knows that he can't go back to work until the strike is over and eventually the argument all blows over. I sometimes feel as though I want to walk out of the house when we have arguments but I know that my mum and dad must feel the same.

When I used to go home from school I used to watch the television but now my dad makes me turn it off and tells me that we have got to keep the electricity bills low. That sometimes causes an argument and I blame it on him for being on strike. Really I know that it's not fair because he is only doing what the rest of the miners are doing because he doesn't want to let the miners' union down.

Since the strike has been on my dad has done a lot more work round the house and now he realises how hard it is for my mum to go out to work and then come home and start doing the housework. It is also a big help to my mum to be able to come home and not to have to start doing the work, because she is able to relax and does not get tired and then she is in a better mood with my dad and my brother.

The strike has also affected me because normally my brother and I go to karate twice a week. At the end of three months we normally take our next belt, but we have only been going to karate once a week so we have not been able to get enough training to go for our higher belt. We have had to stay on our brown and white belt whereas we could have got our black belts by now if we had been training more.

I have also been affected by the strike because at Christmas my brother and I will not get any presents and I won't be able to buy as many presents for my friends so I hope the strike is over before Christmas.

Cheryl Brook, 16, Yorkshire

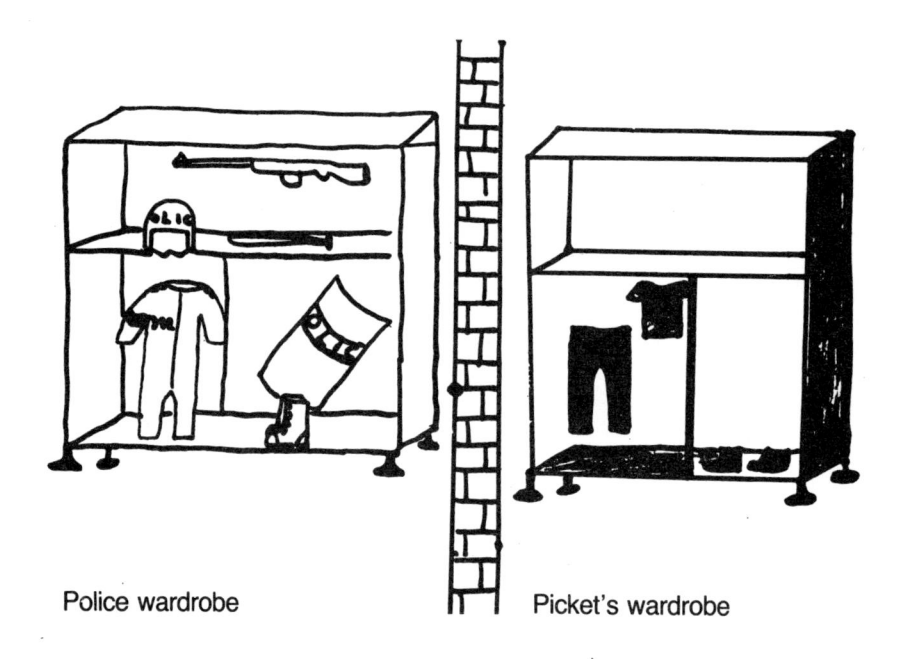

Police wardrobe   Picket's wardrobe

Colin Scott, 15, Northumberland

My views on the strike

My dad was on strike for a year. We have suffered a lot of hardship because we haven't been able to do the things we would have liked to have done. A lot of people couldn't afford to pay their bills etc. I have met a lot of people which has been great. Our friends were the people who were on strike and who supported us. There was a lot of police brutality. This one night a picket was just standing on the picket line just talking to his friends. This policeman came up and grabbed him. The picket tried to struggle and free himself because he didn't know what he had done. The police had fractured his arm, so in the early hours of the morning the police had to take him to hospital. This is just one case I have told you about. There are many more like him. I will never like another policeman again because of what has happened through the strike. I think all the people that were on strike and their wives and families and the people who supported us were wonderful for what they have done through the strike. These are the people you should be proud of, not the scabs. The striking miners can hold their heads up high and say they went on strike to save the mines, not like the scabs who went to work to give them away. I think that nobody will forget the 1984-85 strike because it is something that sticks in your mind for the rest of your life and your children's. I wish that there was a lot more people like them because the world would be a lot more happier place to live in.

From a proud striking miner's child.
Tracey Mabley, 16, Staffordshire

Miners

The miners' strike's gone on too long,
Ian MacGregor I think is wrong.
Peace talks here, peace talks there,
And the scabs, they get their share.
Arthur Scargill, he's all right.
The pickets and bobbies have a fight.
Barricades of fire at Yorkshire mines.
When Mac's around, the sun won't shine.
Maggie, Maggie, she's behind it all,
Maggie out, Maggie out,
Is what the pickets will call.
Castlehill pit is breaking up,
Other pits will probably shut.
Danny McNab, 10, Scotland

Leanne Platek, 11, Staffordshire

54

55

My father's struggle

As I see it the strike came about due to the National Coal Board wanting to close some 'uneconomic' pits, thus putting 20,000 men out of work. The workers from Cortonwood Colliery called the National Union of Mineworkers to call a National Pit Strike. Arthur Scargill called for a strike and got mass support from his men except in Nottinghamshire. Here nearly all the men are working and if this area was shut down the strike would probably stay solid.

Mr Ian MacGregor says these 'uneconomic' pits have to close as they lose money every year. Mr Ray Chadburn and his delegates of the NUM say that the men in Nottinghamshire will not come out on strike unless a national ballot of all members proves to be in favour of a strike.

Personally I think the NUM were right to call a strike in the interests of the workers in the mines. I think though that the Nottinghamshire area should have come out on strike, as now if they wanted a strike it would definitely be unsuccessful as they would get no backing from any other delegates.

The strike has affected me in the manner that is now quite common. My father is on strike on behalf of the other workers in the Union who have been mining the so-called 'uneconomic pits'. My father is not a flying picket and I'm glad he isn't, as for two or three pounds a day you could get your car damaged, beaten up or even arrested for doing nothing. My father gets no money, only so much social security money with which he pays off bills and gives it to my mother to buy food with.

I think the media coverage is all biased against the miners. The police are seen as good guys and the miners completely the opposite. There are also cases of police violence but they will probably get away with their actions.

The papers are all biased against the miners as their owners support the Conservative government. Also the BBC depend on government money so they are biased against the miners so as not to break relations.

I don't think the strike is fair because if the pits were closed then mining communities would break up. If the pits around here closed and my father was transferred then I would have to leave my school, friends and our house just to live somewhere else in the country.

Christmas will definitely be different as the presents will be cheaper and scarcer, so we (me and my sister, that is) will have to be happy and grateful for what we get.

Craig Chambers, 15, Yorkshire

Jason Stewart, 7, Yorkshire

The strike

Food

Our food has changed a lot, mainly because we can't afford it on the money we get each week. When we have paid off the money on the bills (which we pay each week) we are left with about £5. Our Sunday dinner has changed a lot. We still manage to have our Sunday dinner but not steak like we used to have. I have free school meals at school during the week. This isn't a lot and sometimes not very nice but I put up with it. When I come home from school we usually eat soup, beans on toast etc., tinned food. STEAK and CHIPS, NO! Beans on toast. We used to have a big cooked meal three times a week but now only once a week on Sunday.

While I have my school meal my mam and dad go down to the local soup kitchen.

Clothes

I haven't had any new clothes since the beginning of the strike. I have grown out of clothes which I had before the strike. We are lucky we have got my grandma and grandad supporting us. My grandad, a retired miner, bought me two pairs of jeans at Easter. I have grown out of one pair of them but still wear them as ¾ jeans. In September 1984 we had a letter to go to the Y.B.O. in Doncaster to get free clothing but you could only get two things for school. I got a new school skirt and cardigan. In July off the council we got a £10 voucher for a pair of shoes. They have worn down a lot and didn't last very long. My mam and dad couldn't afford to buy me another pair so they had to ask the union if they could possibly buy me a pair and they did, but they have started to wear down.

Picketing
My dad goes picketing every day. He usually goes with Alan and Billy. He shouldn't go picketing now because he has been arrested, but he does. He is to go to court on 19 December 1984. I go to school each day wondering what is happening to my dad. Will he be home tonight when I go home? Quite a few times my dad has come home with bruises on his arms and legs (more bruises than what I get in hockey). My mam has been picketing at our local pit quite a lot when she found out three or four men were going into the pit. Once when she went to picket at Calverton she got arrested. She was found guilty for obstruction and threatening behaviour but was not fined. The other day when my dad came home and told us what had happened during the day I burst out laughing because of the bus which the working men go to work on. About ten peole who got behind the bus said that there was nobody on it and on the back seat they saw cardboard cut-outs of what were supposed to be working men. So somebody on the picket line said (with a policeman next to him): 'We'll bring some cardboard cut-outs with us on the picket line tomorrow and if the cops ask us why we've got them there we'll reply, if you can do it, so can we!'

School
Some of our teachers are very kind now the strike is on. Our games teacher is kind to us. If you have grown out of your kit she asks you if you are a miner's child. If you are she lets you just wear a plain white tee-shirt. My friend Donna Hogg is also a miner's child and hasn't got an art book for art, so she told the teacher she couldn't do her homework because she never had any paper so the teacher gave her a lot of paper. When somebody hasn't got a pen for school and the teacher says you should have a pen, everybody shouts out, "Can't afford it, pit's on strike!"

Christmas
As Christmas time is coming up again my mam and dad are getting worried. The other week I went to Liverpool to a party which some supporters of the strike put on and I got a present of a jewelry box and a watch. My friends at school have bought me a Christmas present. We are also getting presents off the family. I am hoping to get some ankle-boots for Christmas but I don't think I will get any because they cost about £20, but my mam just doesn't have the money.

I am very glad that my mam and dad are fighting for their future and for mine and the other younger generation.

Joanne Green, 13, Yorkshire

Sunjay Maisuria, 7, Hackney, London

We don't want the dole

We don't want the dole
We don't want your lies
We want the right to work
We don't want excuses
We want a future
Or would that really hurt
Our minds are made up
We'll go down fighting
We'll show you what we think
Keep your dole
And Training Schemes
Unemployment stinks
So come on Brothers
Let us unite
Let's show them who we are
A Tory Government
What a Laugh
A future is better by far.
Ellie Bence, Kent

Reason why

O come ye miners
Come follow me
In the greatest fight
That will ever be.

For men to work
And wheels to turn
Can't the people understand
We're fighting for them each in their turn.

To keep communities alive
And not to leave them dead
To keep them buzzing
As ARTHUR SCARGILL said.
Kerry Adele Evans, 12, Wales

In support

Welcome to the Notts miners

We put a big sign up in the hall of our school and it said, 'Welcome to the Notts Miners'. We had Punch and Judy, Doctor Smarty Pants and a big party in the hall. The miners' children came and we played. One boy had a funny badge. It was a little clown saying, 'If Thatcher gets up your nose, picket.' Some of the children said they weren't allowed to talk about the strike in their school. The newspapers said our school put little children out on the street for Arthur Scargill, which is silly. Then an inspector came to our school, and the teachers were worried. There shouldn't be any inspectors — all the children and all the grown-ups in the school should be the inspectors.

Anna Winter, 5, Hackney, London

The miners are on strike

The miners are on strike because Mrs Thatcher said they can't do no work under the ground, and the miners got angry. When the miners got angry they wanted some clothes because they were freezing. They needed some food because they were hungry. How can we win? We can win but they need some money. The police hit the miners. I wasn't surprised. They hit Brian. They arrested the miners. I wasn't surprised. The police sent Zeynep and Fatih back to Turkey. So I know they arrest people. I think they are never fair. I don't know why. Some of the miners were in hospital for a very long time and some went to prison. They didn't do anything wrong. I don't know why they are in prison — it makes me feel awful. I saw it on television. My mum was sad. My dad was very surprised that the miners were in jail. He said this is a terrible thing to happen just because the miners got cross with Mrs Thatcher.

Dale Bryden, 7, Hackney, London

Does Arthur approve?

The house is in mourning, death all around
Silent, there is no sound.
The news came at three o'clock.
We guessed the result, but it still came as a shock.
Families suffering, the men's grief
It also brought relief.
Suddenly a young voice sadly says,
'They make it sound as if we've lost Mam,
Surely Dad isn't going back?
He'll be a scab, we can't have that.'
I try to explain, it's so hard
To someone so young and scared.
'But, does Arthur approve?' he asks.
I explain once again that Arthur really does approve.
For he knows our sufferings are eased, our Union's secure.
We are not going back because our battle is lost.
Fresh we go back, strong, to begin our fight anew.
Tears in his eyes, he turns away and says,
'As long as Arthur really does approve
And Dad's not a scab.'

Doreen Selway, Wales

F12/85

Leningrad
6 March, 1985

Dear friends,

I am not a child, I am 37, and not even a miner's son. But being neither is not my fault — I cannot help it. Just as I cannot help being sympathetic with the British miners' unprecedented perseverance in fighting for their rights.

The poem I am enclosing is a feeble attempt to express this sympathy. I was deeply touched by Ellie Bence's openhearted lines in the *Morning Star* of 19 February ('Supporting Miners is Kids' Stuff'). They reminded me, as it were, of the events in Gordon Parker's book *The Darkness of the Morning* which I read some time ago.

My daughter Barbara is just a little baby now, and I hope she will grow to be as devoted to her father as Ellie is to hers. From our papers I have learnt that the strike is to be finished. As I understand it, it does not mean a defeat. With the most sincere wishes of victory to your miners.

Vitaly Sobolev

P.S. The first lines in the poem are true. I come originally from Karaganda, a town of collieries in Kazakhstan.

I come from a coal-mining town
So far away from your land
That the sun here sinking down
Throws full light on your fist-clenched hand.

You're a pitman like many I know,
And I know how a pitman can fight —
Days go by, by and by weeks go,
You're on strike, your supporters unite.

Some are waiting for you to surrender,
But the workers are your kith and kin,
And the item high on the agenda
Is not whether, but when you're to win!